What Your Handwriting Says About You

What Your Handwriting Says About You

Mike Edelhart

Prentice-Hall, Inc.,
Englewood Cliffs, N.J.

Copyright © 1979 by Mike Edelhart
All rights reserved. No part of this book may be
reproduced in any form or by any means, except for
the inclusion of brief quotations in a review,
without permission in writing from the publisher.
Printed in the United States of America   J
Prentice-Hall International, Inc., London
Prentice-Hall of Australia, Pty. Ltd., North Sydney
Prentice-Hall of Canada, Ltd., Toronto
Prentice-Hall of India Private Ltd., New Delhi
Prentice-Hall of Japan, Inc., Tokyo
Prentice-Hall of Southeast Asia Pte. Ltd., Singapore
Whitehall Books Limited, Wellington, New Zealand
1   2   3   4   5   6   7   8   9   10

Library of Congress Cataloging in Publication Data
Edlehart, Michael.
What your handwriting says about you.
SUMMARY: Provides the reader with basic techniques
in handwriting analysis, presents samples of famous
people to analyze, and discusses the use of analysts and
analysis throughout history and in the field of crime
today.
1. Graphology—Juvenile literature. [1. Graphology]
I. Title.
BF891.E32   155.2'82   79-15331
ISBN 0-13-955302-9

CONTENTS

INTRODUCTION:
The World's Greatest Portrait Gallery 7
SECTION ONE:
The Story of Graphology 11
SECTION TWO:
Let's Analyze Your Handwriting 16
SECTION THREE:
How About a Handwriting Party? 99
SECTION FOUR:
Analyzing the Famous and the Infamous 109
SECTION FIVE
For More Information 115

INDEX 117

INTRODUCTION:

The World's Greatest Portrait Gallery

Some people like football, some like chess. Some people like classical music, others prefer rock and roll.

If someone said to you, "My friend Sue likes baseball and rock, but my friend Jim likes chess and classical music," you would get very different pictures of Jim and Sue in your mind.

The things Sue and Jim like, the things they like to look at and have around them, affect the kind of people they are. And, knowing these likes and dislikes can help you know them.

In the same way, handwriting can tell you things about the personality of the person doing the writing. Some people like their letters to look one way, and some another. Some folks favor sweeping giant-sized letters and others write in tight, precise bunches.

The types of letters people like and the different kinds of loops, lines, and flourishes they use when they write provide glimpses of their personalities.

For generations, experts have studied handwriting and gathered information about which personality traits are reflected in which letters and writing patterns.

Their studies have uncovered strong ties between the way people put words on paper and the way they behave. This work by experts led to the creation of the science of handwriting analysis, called graphology.

Graphology involves predicting facts about people, but it is much different from such magical practices as predicting by numbers (numerology), by the stars (astrology), by cards (Tarot), by sticks (I-Ching), and hundreds of other means.

These magical, or occult, sciences work with mystical forces, spirits, and other strange phenomena. But graphology deals with real objects. The writer's pen is real, so is the paper. The letters on the page are real and the movements used to make them were real, as well.

So, the findings of graphology aren't really predictions at all. They are conclusions drawn from the facts the writer has hidden in the way he forms his handwriting.

Handwriting analysis is a very natural way to get an impression of a personality. If you can tell a lot about a person by the books on his library shelves—which are nothing more than words the person likes or admires—how much more you can find out through his writing, which is words he likes expressed in the most personal way possible.

What Handwriting Analysis Reveals

Handwriting doesn't predict, it reveals. A graphologist can't actually see the future in someone's handwriting. It merely reflects personality traits. But these traits may influence how a person lives his life and how he reacts to situations in the future.

Is the writer mean? Is he scared? Is he determined, lazy, smug, content, or criminally insane? Handwriting analysis can tell you these things.

But graphology won't say that someone will meet a tall, dark stranger or marry a prince.

Let's say that Joe's writing reveals that he is determined, talented, self-confident, and intelligent. His handwriting doesn't predict the future, but it does show a person who is likely to be successful in the future.

On the other hand, if Joe's handwriting shows a weak character, laziness, stubbornness, and a tendency toward depression, we can fairly conclude that he will have a hard life and often be unhappy.

You have probably heard someone say, "I'm no artist. I could never paint a picture of myself."

But, when it comes to handwriting, everyone is an artist. In the strokes and curves, the thin lines and thick swirls of handwriting, everyone is painting his own lifelong self-portrait.

We are all artists every time we sit down with a pen and paper. And to those who know the principles of graphology, the whole world is the ultimate art gallery, full of fascinating portraits of everyone in it.

SECTION ONE:

The Story of Graphology

The scientific study of handwriting has only been practiced for about 150 years, but people have been intrigued with the shape and form of their writing as long as there have been letters.

The Ancient Roman book, **Lives of the Caesars,** for instance, discussed ties between writing and personality. And one of those Caesars, Nero, is said to have been seriously interested in the subject.

A theory of handwriting and personality was first stated by the Frenchman Francis Demelles in 1609. In the years that followed handwriting study became a huge fad.

Such famous authors as Robert Browning, Baudelaire, and John Keats all dabbled in handwriting analysis. And the German master Goethe wrote that "in every man's writings, the character of the writer must lie recorded."

Another famous writer who became convinced that handwriting held secrets was the poet Sir Walter Scott who once said "...I could not help thinking, according to an opinion I have heard seriously maintained, that something of a man's character may be conjectured from his handwriting."

The true birth of graphology, however, came around 1860, when two French monks, Abbe Flandrin and Abbe Jean Hippolyte Michon, began collecting huge files of handwriting samples and studying them for common characteristics. Abbe Michon invented the word "graphology" to describe their work and published the first major books in the field.

At the end of the 19th Century, Germany took over the lead in graphology through the work of Dr. Ludwig Klages, a philosopher whose five books on handwriting analysis form the basis for the modern science.

Germany remains the center of graphology today. Handwriting study is included in many German medical school courses. Psychologists and doctors can become certified graphologists through a tough three-year study program.

In America, on the other hand, graphology has not been so widely accepted. To many, it has seemed merely a clever parlor game, not a true science. Still, graphology has played an interesting role in American criminology and business.

Graphologists have become involved in many of this century's most celebrated court cases. During the infamous Lindbergh kidnapping case, for example, a major newspaper chain hired graphologist Milton Bunker to examine the writing of Bruno Hauptman. Hauptman had been accused of abducting and killing the child of flying hero Charles Lindbergh. He swore he was innocent.

The paper wanted to see if his handwriting revealed any clues. Bunker's study convinced him of the strong possibility that Hauptman was telling the truth. But he was convicted and electrocuted for the crime, anyway.

In the more recent Son of Sam killings in New York and the Zodiac murder spree in San Francisco, handwriting analysts were employed to help create pictures of the killers' personalities from notes they had written.

Courts sometimes use handwriting analysts to compare signatures on important documents and to testify about a person's state of mind while he wrote a particular passage.

In business, graphology is becoming an important tool for selecting employees. Some 2,000 American companies use graphologists as consultants, according to the International Graphoanalysis Society.

Companies also use handwriting analysis to uncover crooked workers. In one case, Father Norman Werling, a graphologist and priest from New Jersey, was called in to investigate widespread credit card fraud at a gas station. His examination of a worker's handwriting convinced a judge to issue a search warrant which led to the arrest of a night manager for the crime.

You probably won't be able to achieve such dramatic results to begin with, but you should realize that examining handwriting is more than a game. It is an age-old tradition which has important modern applications.

If you practice hard and become very good at graphology, you might even be able to analyze writing for a living some day.

SECTION TWO:

Let's Analyze Your Handwriting

The best way to learn about graphology is to practice on yourself. By examining a sample of your own writing, you can find out new things about your personality while you master the basic techniques of graphology.

Here's how you start: Take one clean sheet of unlined white paper and whichever kind of pen you prefer. Without giving yourself too much time to think it over, sit down and write a page-full of whatever comes into your head.

It can be a letter, a make-believe speech, or just line after line of nonsense. Don't write poetry—it's not natural and takes too much thought to let your writing be natural. And, most of all, don't try to make your writing look **pretty**. This isn't a penmanship quiz, it's an attempt to discover what your everyday writing reveals about you. So, don't hide yourself behind a gussied-up style.

In any case, faked handwriting tends to increase your natural peculiarities rather than hide them. So you might as well let it all hang out.

When you've filled the page, sign it.

Once you have your sample in hand you're ready to practice graphology!

The Preliminary Examination

We analyze handwriting beginning with the most general characteristics and working down to the most specific—the lines and curves of individual letters. Many indications can be found at each level. Often, findings in different parts of the analysis don't agree. This is no problem. No one is entirely consistent. We are all richly complex, which is what makes us, as a species, so wonderful.

It is vital, also, that you remember that no indication equals a pronouncement. If you see a characteristic in your writing that is common in criminals, it doesn't mean you're going to become Jack the Ripper. A handwriting analysis consists of many, many observations laid on top of one another. The ones that appear most often are the dominant themes of the personality. Others provide degrees of shading. None is all-important.

In other words, don't jump to conclusions. Complete the examination carefully and study the results soberly before you draw any inferences from your writing. Remember, graphology is a science. Like crime detection it uses many small clues to build an impressive case. But no single clue can stand alone.

Zones

First, we're going to look at how your writing fits into zones. Take a sheet of ruled notebook paper and lay it over your writing sample so that a rule lies directly beneath the letters of one line you've written, like this:

The space just above this rule is the **middle zone.** The space below it is the **lower zone.** And the space above the first rule upward is the **upper zone.**

19

Most letters fall entirely in the middle zone:

The taller letters rise into the upper zone:

The tailed letters dip into the lower zone:

Each zone represents different areas of personality, affected by the way the letters are formed in the zone.

The **upper zone** is the reflection of intellectual or abstract pursuits.

The **middle zone** reflects the day-to-day visible personality and actions of the writer.

The **lower zone** reveals desires, drives, urges, and compulsions.

When any zone is emphasized in handwriting it means the person has particularly strong leanings in that area.

Look at these two examples:

to be or not to be

The time of my life

The first is a person who tries to squeeze every letter into the middle zone. This person is rooted in the work-a-day world, social relationships, habits, and basically doing what is expected without questions.

The second person is a real dreamer. The more exaggerated the upper zone loops, the more imaginative the writer. This person is also rather driven, perhaps even show-offish because of the plunging loops in the lower zone.

Here are some other characteristics to look for in the zones of your own writing:

A person who de-emphasizes the middle zone probably doesn't pay much attention to daily routine. A brilliant, absent-minded professor might write this way:

historical records show a perfectly

In the upper zone, full loops denote an interest in creativity. The simpler the loop, the more down-to-earth the creative form is likely to be:

*Thomas
holly*

Avoidance of the upper zone indicates disinterest in mental pursuits:

he pulled the trolley

The narrower the upper zone loops the more cautious the attitude toward mental pursuits. Very narrow loops can mean lack of imagination, if not offset by other signs, which we'll talk about later:

if he tries anything, ell

A full lower zone with closed loops indicates a person interested in public attention, a performance, body-oriented person:

yearn for a full life

Wide, emphasized lower loops denote highly developed instincts:

going away cto stay

Generally, the odder the lower zone loops, the kinkier physical needs and drives the writer is likely to have:

The pointier the lower loops, the less compromising a person is likely to be:

finding yourself

The length of the lower loop indicates the level of involvement the person attains. If the loops reach the next line, the person may have problems with overidentification with others.

slowly he played, his tones filled

If the loops in the lower zone tighten into lines, the writer is expressing repression. But a strong, single, downward stroke also indicates firmness, leadership:

you fear you

Unfinished loops indicate frustration with sex, position in life, and other drive-centered matters:

try, please try

Basically, the zones tip us off to three possibilities:

The greater the strength of the middle zone, the more world oriented the writer.

The greater the strength of the upper zone, the more intellectual or imaginative the writer.

The greater the strength of the lower zone, the more personal, internally oriented the writer.

Slant

The slant of a handwriting reveals the writer's attitude toward the world. We all begin by writing with the neat, straight-up style of our penmanship books. But then, over the years, our personalities and experiences take over and our letters change.

The degree and direction of slant we give our writing is a clear indication of how we feel about the world we are in.

Here is a chart I call the emotion wheel. You can use it to get a general picture of what your slant says about you. Line up the middle of the chart's bottom line with the base of a "b," "d," "t," or other long letter and compare your slant with the chart readings.

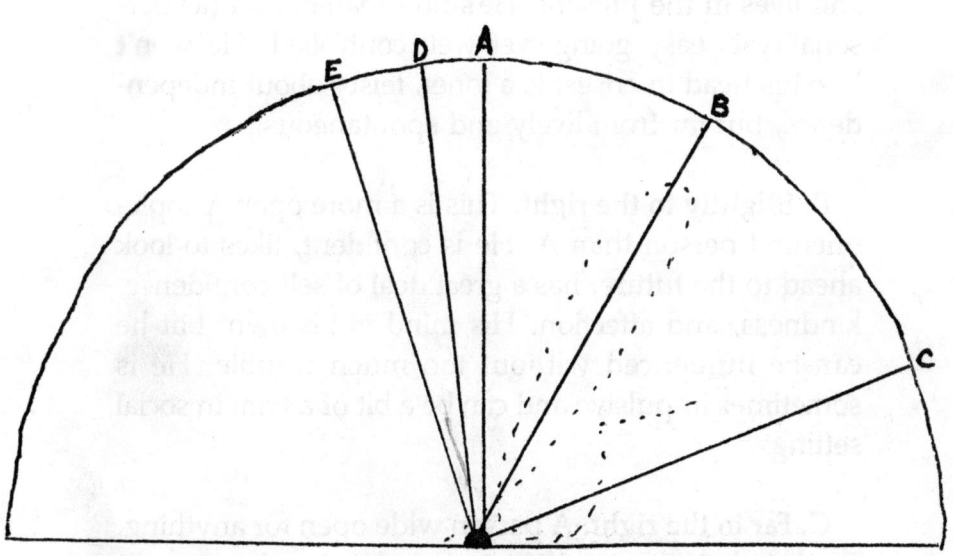

The letters at the end of each line on the chart are the traditional notations for the five types of slant accepted by graphologists. Here are what the slants reveal about the writer:

A. Straight up and down. This person is practical and lives in the present. He's no dreamer and his personality is easy going, yet well controlled. He won't lose his head in crises, is a loner, feisty about independence, but far from lively and spontaneous.

B. Slightly to the right. This is a more open, people-oriented person than A. He is confident, likes to look ahead to the future, has a great deal of self-confidence, kindness, and affection. His mind is his own, but he can be influenced without too much trouble. He is sometimes impulsive and can be a bit of a ham in social settings.

C. Far to the right. A person wide open for anything. Tends to have poor self-control, rushes in where angels fear to tread. He's very intense, expressive, sensitive, and very dependent upon others. But, when crossed, he can become violent with frustration.

D. **Slightly to the left.** This slant reflects less emotional conduct. The writer is thoughtful, self-centered, picky about all personal possessions. He has a high degree of objectivity, almost aloofness. Cold, he has trouble expressing emotions, adapting to new situations; possibly even somewhat alienated and repressed.

E. **Very far left.** Indications here are a badly repressed childhood, feelings of rejection, uncertainty about what lies ahead, disillusion, defiance, defensiveness, social discomfort, and an unrealistic view of life.

Sometimes one person's writing will shift from one slant to another. In general, shifting slants indicate a highly sensitive nature, moodiness, flexibility, an unfocused, changeable attitude toward life, and possible undependability. In addition, the characteristics of the slants that dominate the writing must be weighed in the evaluation.

A second type of slant to look for in your writing is the **directional trend.** The crosses on the "t's," the flourishes at the ends of words and lines, the loops on "Y's" all can have slants of their own. Here is an example:

In this case the loops tend to the left, while most of the writing leans to the right. The left directional trend of these strokes moderates the right leaning influence. If the loops had veered far right they would have increased the effect of the overall right slant.

Look over your writing for the letter slant and directional trend. Note down your findings.

Line Direction

Whole lines, as well as single words, slant in writing. Some people's writing angles up the page, some angles slightly downward. Some people even write in little arcs, with the words in the middle of their lines being the highest.

The direction your handwritten lines take on the page is another element in your graphological self-portrait. See which of these forms most closely fits your writing:

Writing slants up the page. You are optimistic, look forward to the future with a happy heart. You feel loved, enthusiastic, and content.

I am an optimist, as you can see.

Writing slants down the page. Quite the opposite. You are dreary, pessimistic, all tired out. You're down in the dumps, depressed. In short, you've got the blues.

I am not particularly happy right now.

Writing parallel to the edges of the paper. You are everybody's good citizen: reliable, mild-mannered, ruled by your head, not your heart. You are resolute and in full control, but unfortunately, perhaps a mite dull, also.

I am a very reliable person.

Writing that forms on arc. You're a great starter, but a lousy finisher. You are optimistic at the beginning of everything but lose interest and patience before its completion.

I start fast, then slow down.

Writing that forms a dish. The opposite of the person above. You're a slow starter but come through in the end with flying colors. You are the tortoise in "The Hare and the Tortoise."

I start slowly, then pick up steam.

Even line but words each slant downward. You need a lot of encouragement. You have to fight to stay "up." You're basically a solid person, but you have doubts about yourself.

I need encouragement.

Even line, but words each slant upward. You are very optimistic and enthusiastic but perhaps a little too eager and simplistic in your view of the world. You may lack the stamina to match your rosy outlook.

Strokes

We'll examine three kinds of strokes in your writing: connective, beginning, and ending.

Connecting strokes are the lines between letters that make handwriting different from printing. They come in four main patterns:

The Garland:

uuuuuu take the

The Arcade:

nnnnn from home

The Angle:

vvvvvv the time is now for all good

The Thread:

———— *some came running*

Each pattern, of course, has its special meaning. Often, different patterns will appear in one person's writing. This simply means that combinations of characteristics exist in the writer's personality.

Garlands denote adaptability, a distaste for conflict, a sympathetic, outgoing personality. An extrovert.

Some graphologists compare a garland to a cup. The deeper the bow in the garland, the larger the cup that must be filled in the writer's personality, and the more receptive to outside ideas he'll be in order to fill it.

Arcades reflect self-protectiveness, a measured sort of friendliness. This person plays his hand close to his chest, puts emphasis on appearance, but neglects to look beneath surface features.

Angular connectives show a lack of adaptability, rigidity, high ideals, unswervingness. In other words, a very mulish person.

Threads come from people with insight, versatility, intelligence, quick wit. The thread implies putting things together and putting up little resistance against the flow.

The presence or lack of connectives, in general, also has meanings. Basically, the smoother and more prevalent the use of connectives the more logical, steady, persistent, and social the writer will be. The more breaks between letters, the more intuitive, impulsive, inventive, free thinking, nonconformist, and artistic the person is likely to be.

Beginning strokes are a writer's way of expressing his attitude toward new situations. There are an infinite number of possible beginning strokes, but here are the more common ones to compare against your own writing:

Natural curved beginning. An obedient, unimpulsive, cautious sort of person with a healthy respect for the past. Will take some time to adjust to new situations.

take the money and run

Straight beginning. A person with hidden tensions or resentments against the past. Lacks self-assurance and self-confidence. Resists change. The longer the beginning stroke the greater the lure of the past.

take the money and run

Below the base line beginning. Strong subconscious urges, particularly toward success. Impatient, aggressive.

take the money and run

Curly-que beginning. A person who wants to own lots of things. A hoarder or collector.

take the money and run.

Hook beginning. A jealous, possessive person.

take the money and run

Dark spot beginning. Denotes hidden facts in the past the writer does not want revealed.

take the money and run

Underline beginning. Implies extreme self-absorption. A prissy person.

Take the money and run

Upper zone beginning. An enterprising individual, possibly idealistic and religious.

Take the money and run

No beginning stroke. A real go-getter, very efficient, smart, practical, a person who gets things done.

take the money and run

Ending strokes reveal the writer's true social personality, not the way he appears to others, but the way he feels about himself in his dealings with the outside world.

Long curved ending with blunt end. Shows a person of a giving, generous nature.

good day

Uptilted ending with tapering end. A different kind of giver from the above. Would like to see some gain from giving. Not truly selfless.

good day

Final curving back to the left. An introvert, a self-interested person, probably insecure.

good day

High ending. A quester for knowledge. Common in occult enthusiasts.

good day

Blunt ending, unextended. A frank, blunt-talking person.

good day

Straight ending that comes to a point. Unruly, argumentative person. Stubborn and nasty.

good day

No ending stroke. Not likely to do you a favor. Not outgoing, but honest. Quietly self-confident. Doesn't talk much, offer much, or want much in return.

good day

Incomplete ending stroke. Selfish, lazy, doesn't finish projects.

Ending that hooks to the left and down. A grasping, greedy scrooge.

End stroke that curves down and under. A self-centered, tempermental person.

good day

A whiplike ending. Temper

good day

Spacing

We place spaces between our written words much as we do between the words we speak. Some people rush all their words together in a headlong attempt to get them said quickly. Others have huge gaps in their speaking while they try to think of the next word.

The same thing happens when we write. Differing personalities produce differing patterns of spaces on the page. It's not anything we do deliberately, but it is a revealing unconscious action.

Small even spacing is made by the open, talkative, impulsive, condifent, well-balanced, trusting person.

don't be silly

Small irregular spacing is the product of a chatty, outgoing, insecure, gullible personality.

don't be silly

Large regular spacing reflects an introvert who appreciates literature, poetry, and music. He is thoughtful, proud, possibly snobbish, inhibited, and cautious.

don't be silly

Large, uneven spacing shows a critical mind hampered by difficulty in expressing itself. The person is likely to be hesitant or confused in decision making.

don't be silly

Extremely large gaps, which waste paper and the reader's time, indicate an egotist who doesn't care about others, a loner who is pitting himself against the world. If this appears in an otherwise positive sample, it probably means the writer is very frustrated about part of his life, he needs to get away from it all for awhile.

don't be silly

Spacing between lines is another important consideration. Graphologists feel writers consciously measure the distance between their lines, which makes this a good measure of mental organization and conscious attitudes.

Narrow line spacing points toward a spontaneous person without much reserve or objectivity. Also denotes stinginess and possible confusion.

take the time to try it

Tangled spacing is a sign of serious lack of inhibitions, problems with over-involvement, and over-indulgence; a wildly impulsive person.

take the time to try it

Upper zone tangling implies that the writer has daydreams, usually rather racy in content, but never acts them out.

take the time to try it

Wide, even spacing is the mark of the well-mannered, organized, reasonable, person. An executive, perhaps, self-assured, a good planner and leader.

take the time to try it

Extremely wide spacing comes from a desire to be uninvolved and separated from life or reality. The writer is probably lonely.

take the time to try it

Irregular spacing comes from a lack of will power.

take the time to try it

Margins

The placement of writing on the page is yet another telling factor to the graphologist. Examination of the margins around writing reveals attitudes toward tolerance, economy, consistency, and social acceptance.

The **top margin** on the page is the indicator of formality, modesty, and the writer's regard for the reader. The wider the margin, the greater these qualities; the narrower, the weaker.

Left margins show the writer's need for esteem. **Right margins** reveal how close the writer actually lets others get to him.

Here are some possible margin combinations and what they stand for:

Wide left-wide right. The left is a sign of high standards, a deep cultural background, self-respect, little need for others, even shyness. The right shows fears of what lies ahead, an unrealistic attitude, sensitivity, perhaps extravagance, extreme need for neatness, a high level of aloofness.

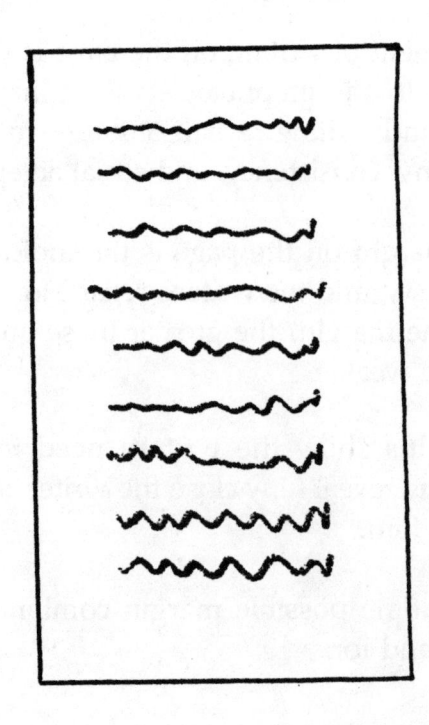

Extra wide left-narrow right. The left denotes the writer's refusal to look at himself realistically. He has great reserve, almost defensive snobbism. Many people with bad childhoods or divorces write this way. The narrow right indicates a desire for closeness with others, acceptance. The person is probably very sociable, a good talker and mixer at parties.

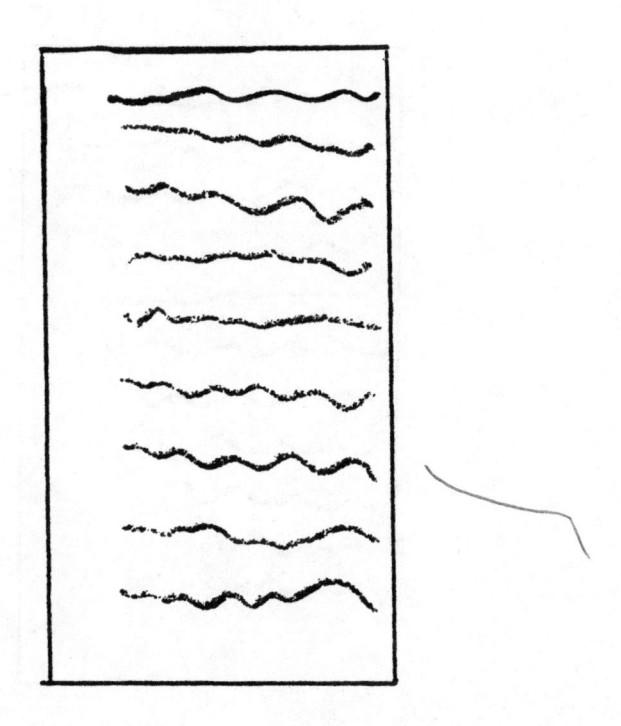

Narrow left-widening right. The narrow left is chosen by someone craving familiarity, popularity, recognition. Probably has a free and easy style in public. The widening right points toward fear that others might not respond to the writer as he hopes.

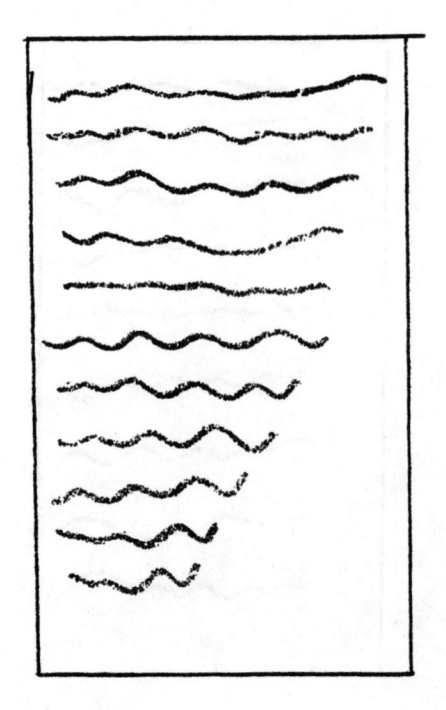

Widening left-narrowing right. The left is a mark of hastiness, increasing lavishness, poor spending habits, impatience, and galloping enthusiasm. The right shows growing self-confidence, waning shyness as situations progress.

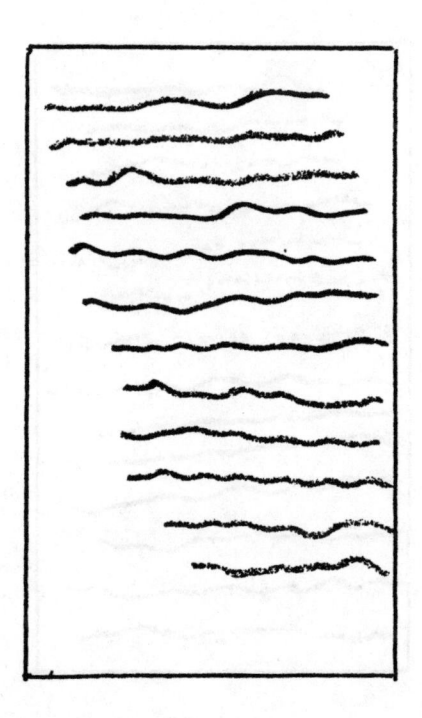

Narrowing left-uneven right. Shyness, unsocialability, withdrawal, bad money sense, possible depression, and illness are the conclusions based on the left. The right points up thriftlessness, as well as a love of travel and changeable attitudes.

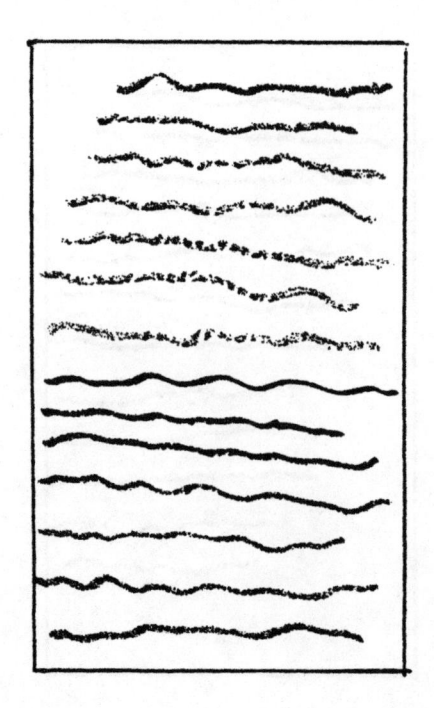

Even left-even right. The left points toward discipline, good manners, and a desire to do things properly. The right is a sign of stiffness, self-consciousness, and conformity.

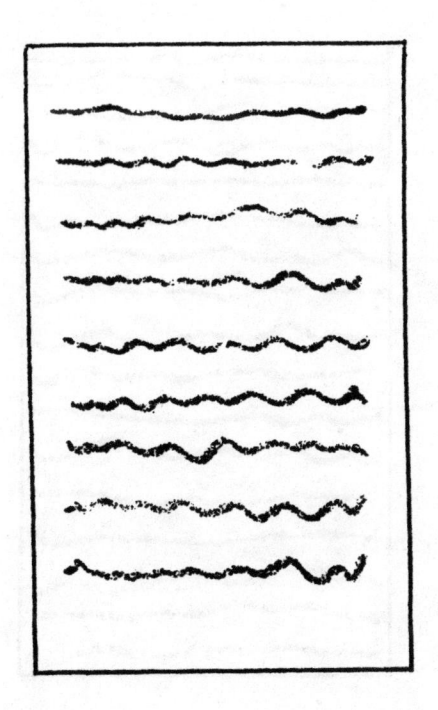

Narrow all around. Depending upon other readings, this can picture a person of miserliness, tactlessness, sympathy, charity, and graciousness who desires many possessions, much luxury, and enjoys morbid thrills.

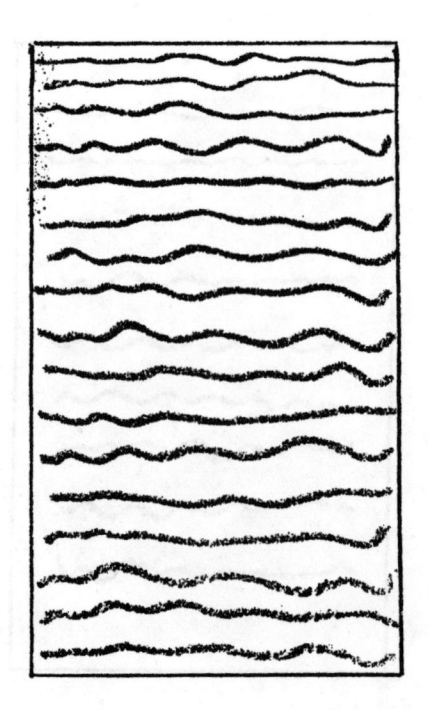

Very wide all around. A lonely, withdrawn, spiritual, secretive sort of person. A hermit.

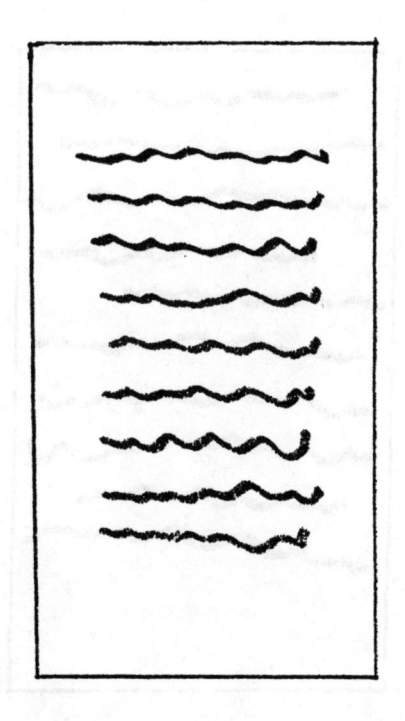

Uneven all around. A disorganized but versatile individual. Tolerant of others, careless, and inattentive.

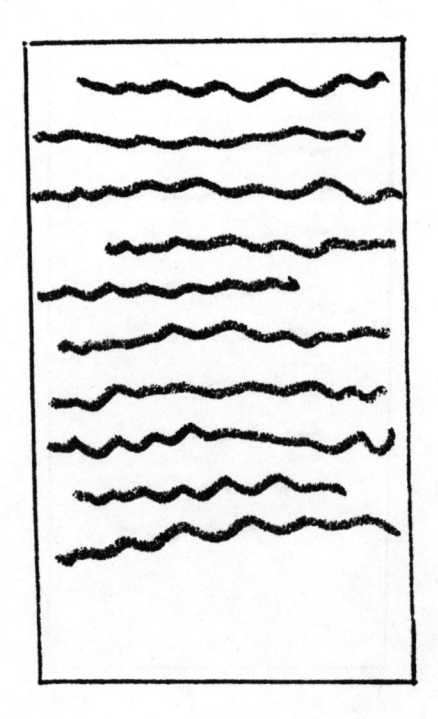

Pressure

A recent commercial for BIC Banana pens talked about all the different ways you could write with one for different situations. For a tough letter a wide, bold stroke. For a love note, a thin, pretty line.

The strength of the lines we write is largely the result of pressure. Some of us press very hard, others barely caress the page with the pen tip.

To a graphologist, pressure is an excellent measure of intensity, vitality, and forcefulness. It is an unconscious habit that reveals the strength of the writer's urges.

Heavy pressure can be both seen and felt. Feel the back of the sheet. The depth of the impression made by your pen or pencil gives you an idea of how much pressure was applied. With a felt-tipped pen, pressure translates into darkness and line depth.

As the paper soaks up the ink pressed on it by heavy pressure, the writer soaks up experience, translates it to his own needs, and stores it for future use. He has enormous endurance, great drive, and enthusiasm. He is creative, physically expressive, and deeply committed to his emotions. He remembers wrongs for a long time and holds a grudge. He prefers dark or bright colors and rich foods.

Forward Into The Breach!

Extra heavy pressure shows vanity, illness, or secretiveness, and sometimes depression.

I don't know what to do

Light pressure is the mark of the sensitive, but not dynamic, person. He forgives quickly, wants to avoid friction and fights at all costs. Physically, he may be weak, emotionally he is tender and intuitive. He likes pastel colors and light foods.

Love to all eternal

Changing pressure is a sign of internal turmoil, inferiority feelings, emotional conflict.

Please don't take me for granted

If the pressure on the left side of loops disappears, you can suspect fear of the past. If it disappears on the right side, fear of the future.

he hurried along

Pasty writing uses pressure artistically, mixing thick lines and filled-in spaces to create a studied effect with the words. When pasty writing is neat and regular it indicates highly positive traits: artistic nature, great perception, a winning personality, a highly developed set of senses. Basically, someone warm, charming, and good to know.

When pasty writing is so filled in it becomes illegible, the writer may be considered undisciplined, lazy, undependable, unsteady, secretive, and generally out of step with the universe. Criminals show this trait often.

When The Moon Is Full

Size

Now, at last, we get down to the letters themselves. The first consideration with letters is size. Basically, the size of a writer's letters and the size of the share he expects from life correspond. Size denotes the writer's self-esteem.

We will look at four main types of writing sizes: tall, small, broad, and narrow. If middle zone letters average less than two millimeters in height, the writing is considered small. If they are more than three millimeters high, the writing is considered tall or large.

Tall writing shows a person reaching for the heights. He is ambitious, craves approval, a strong general observer but poor at detail. He may lack consideration, modesty, and tact, but he likes himself very much, all the same.

live happily

Small writing is the product of a person who takes everything apart and looks at it closely before acting. He is modest and reserved, doesn't show himself off. The smaller the writing, the more intellectual the writer.

If the small writing is angular, with print-like capitals, the writer has a scientific bent, is a deep reader and keen thinker.

Small writers are brainy, conservative, and not overly confident.

Wide writing implies a person who needs lots of personal space. He is a rover, a traveler, a self-oriented individual. He likes to spend on himself and boast. He likes being friendly as long as he gets the same or better in return. Discretion, discipline, and tact may be lacking, but the person is frank, natural, and imaginative.

I live all over

Narrow writing comes from a feeling of being hemmed in by life. The person displays inhibitions, great self-discipline, and economy. He conserves everything in his life, from love to money. He may be socially dull and somewhat distrustful of others.

I live all over town

Tall letters all packed into the middle zone show a longing for fame or greatness, hero worship, eccentricity, and love of food.

the road to the top

Irregular letter size shows emotional unevenness. The writer might be zany or moody, quick tempered or even violent.

if he goes down to defeat

The size of capital letters should be examined separately. Look for these notable patterns in your writing:

Tall, narrow capitals stem from feelings of self-importance and coolness to others.

Melvin Jones

Capitals that slant down to the right are signs of a diplomatic person, who perhaps looks down on others in his heart.

Joey Rubin

Tall, dominant capitals show artistic temperament, imagination, and a puffed-up self-image that may mask deep inferiority feelings.

Max Kramer

Capitals that slant up to the right stem from immaturity and a gap between outward confidence and inner shakiness.

Marsha Brand

Simplification

Now we're going to check for how simplified your writing is. Simplification means that only the essential lines are used to create letters. The writer boils everything down to a personal code that is still legible to others.

Generally, simplified writing is a sign of high intelligence and practical state of mind. These examples show you different kinds of simplified writing:

you and I are big kids

How simple are your letters? Do you use few lines or are there many swirls, loops, and other embellishments?

Simplification can be carried to an unreadable extreme, which is called neglected writing. Neglected writing can mean many things. If the writer seems to be writing fast, leaving letters out in the process, it may be because his rush of thoughts outstrips his ability to put them down.

On the other hand, a slowly written, neglected style could indicate a writer so wrapped up in his thoughts and plans that he is neglecting the necessary task of communication.

tomorrow is another day

The opposite of simplification is enrichment. An enriched style writer seeks beauty and loveliness. In enriched writing the words and letters become an artistic expression of the writer's personality. The style fills the entire writing sample, giving it a consistent character and feel.

Enriched, broad, pasty writing is the artist's style. Enriched writing with poor spacing notes a person overimpressed with trifles. Enriched writing that has been labored over shows an idle person, all show and no substance. Enriched writing where lines overlap and the layout is messy implies a fussy, forgetful person.

please try something

The most negative writing style is fragmentary. Here, only parts of letters are written. The downstroke of a small "t", for instance, may be present with the upstroke totally missing. This is a style of mental disorder, eccentricity, and fanaticism. Basically, the writer is saying through his writing that he wants to sever all ties with the world.

The Alphabet

At this point you have looked at your writing's zones, strokes, margins, size, style, pressure, and slant. Now comes the careful examination of individual letters.

We are all taught a standard way to write, but, after a few years, all of us change every letter to suit ourselves. Tiny differences in the way we make each letter can announce vast differences in our characters.

The graphological examination of letters is like breaking a code. The words on the page relate our conscious message. But hidden in the lines, curls, and openings in each letter is a secret message about ourselves and our feelings about life.

Here, in these examples of different letter types, is the key to breaking the code of your handwriting:

A. A expresses the degree of honesty, openness, and sociability.

A A A — fatherly, protective; known as the Lincoln A.

a — modesty (capital as enlarged small letter)

A — subordinated (low cross stem)

W — hard boiled, resentful (angled tips)

A a — chatty, stretches the truth (open top)

A a — The narrower the capital, the shier the writer.

A — Inner knot denotes family and self pride.

X — Offbeat, hasty, imprecise.

a — trustworthy, reserved, closemouthed (closed top)

a — talkative, open to others (open top)

a — a little dishonest (knot on left)

a — rationalizer, hides truth from self (knot on right)

a — dishonest with self and others (double knot)

a — skimpy knots show a person who tells little white lies.

a — friendly, but not always truthful (knotted and open)

a — tells tales about himself, makes himself more than he is. (overstroke)

a — hung up on sex (inner hook)

a — pathological liar (inner pointed hood)

a — greedy despite surface appearances (check mark final)

a — no moral values; known as embezzler's oval. (Open bottom)

a a — self interest, cunning, shiftiness (scrolls, circles)

76

B. **B** is a letter of expression, communication with others.

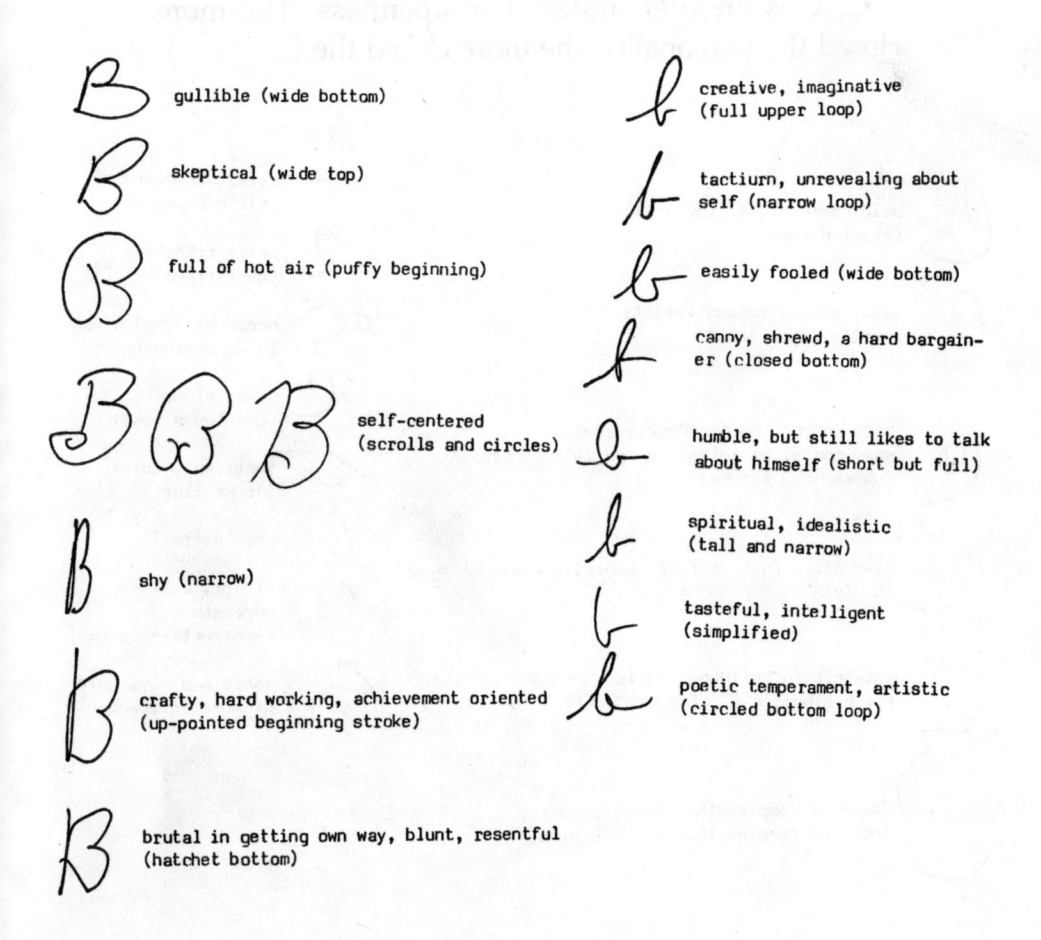

gullible (wide bottom)

skeptical (wide top)

full of hot air (puffy beginning)

self-centered (scrolls and circles)

shy (narrow)

crafty, hard working, achievement oriented (up-pointed beginning stroke)

brutal in getting own way, blunt, resentful (hatchet bottom)

creative, imaginative (full upper loop)

tactiurn, unrevealing about self (narrow loop)

easily fooled (wide bottom)

canny, shrewd, a hard bargainer (closed bottom)

humble, but still likes to talk about himself (short but full)

spiritual, idealistic (tall and narrow)

tasteful, intelligent (simplified)

poetic temperament, artistic (circled bottom loop)

C. C is another indicator of openness. The more closed the personality, the more closed the C.

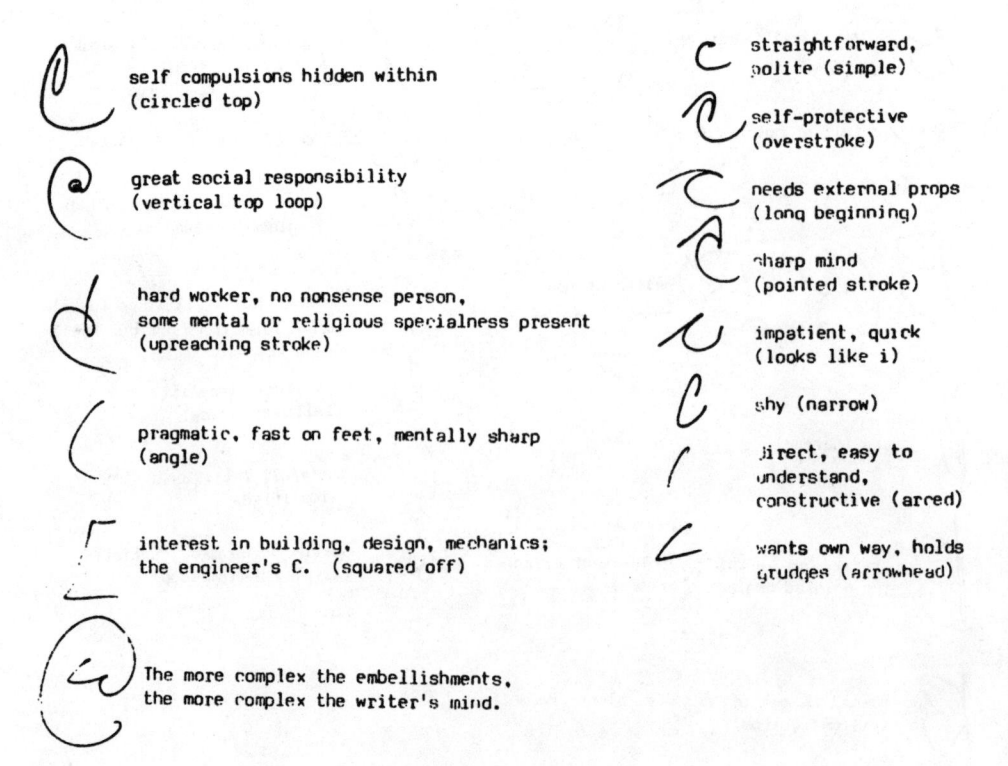

self compulsions hidden within
(circled top)

great social responsibility
(vertical top loop)

hard worker, no nonsense person,
some mental or religious specialness present
(upreaching stroke)

pragmatic, fast on feet, mentally sharp
(angle)

interest in building, design, mechanics;
the engineer's C. (squared off)

The more complex the embellishments,
the more complex the writer's mind.

straightforward,
polite (simple)

self-protective
(overstroke)

needs external props
(long beginning)

sharp mind
(pointed stroke)

impatient, quick
(looks like i)

shy (narrow)

direct, easy to
understand,
constructive (arced)

wants own way, holds
grudges (arrowhead)

78

D. D relates to conduct, dress, and creativity.

intelligence, good taste
(simplified)

feels great self-importance
(full arc, extended understroke)

feels out of place in society, misanthropic
(unconnected parts)

self-centered
(embellished)

secretive, self-reliant
(closed top)

easy talker, social person
(open top)

flirtatious
(flying final stroke)

overblown ego
(extremely wide)

doesn't reveal inner self
(closed bottom)

talks about himself easily
(open bottom)

untrustworthy, a crook
(break in bottom stroke)

meager self-image
(low stem)

proud, idealistic
(tall stem)

flirtatious, poetic, artistic;
so-called Greek style
(simple, creative, flying final)

mentally lazy
(two-part final stroke)

good listener, receptive
(two lines of loop traced over
each other)

touchy, sensitive
(wide upper loop)

suits truth to situation,
diplomatic (knotted)

protective of self, likes
music (leftward overstroke)

E. E expresses feelings of self-image.

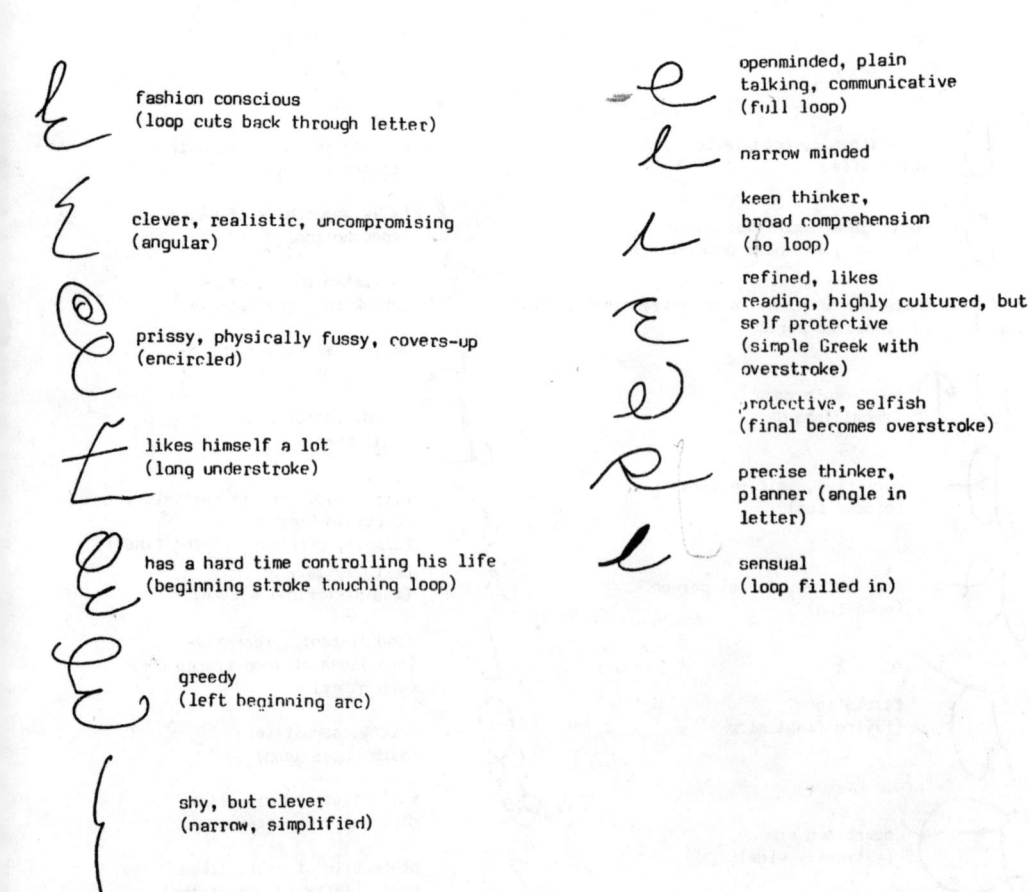

fashion conscious
(loop cuts back through letter)

clever, realistic, uncompromising
(angular)

prissy, physically fussy, covers-up
(encircled)

likes himself a lot
(long understroke)

has a hard time controlling his life
(beginning stroke touching loop)

greedy
(left beginning arc)

shy, but clever
(narrow, simplified)

openminded, plain talking, communicative
(full loop)

narrow minded

keen thinker,
broad comprehension
(no loop)

refined, likes reading, highly cultured, but self protective
(simple Greek with overstroke)

protective, selfish
(final becomes overstroke)

precise thinker, planner (angle in letter)

sensual
(loop filled in)

F. F reflects the level of planning ability.

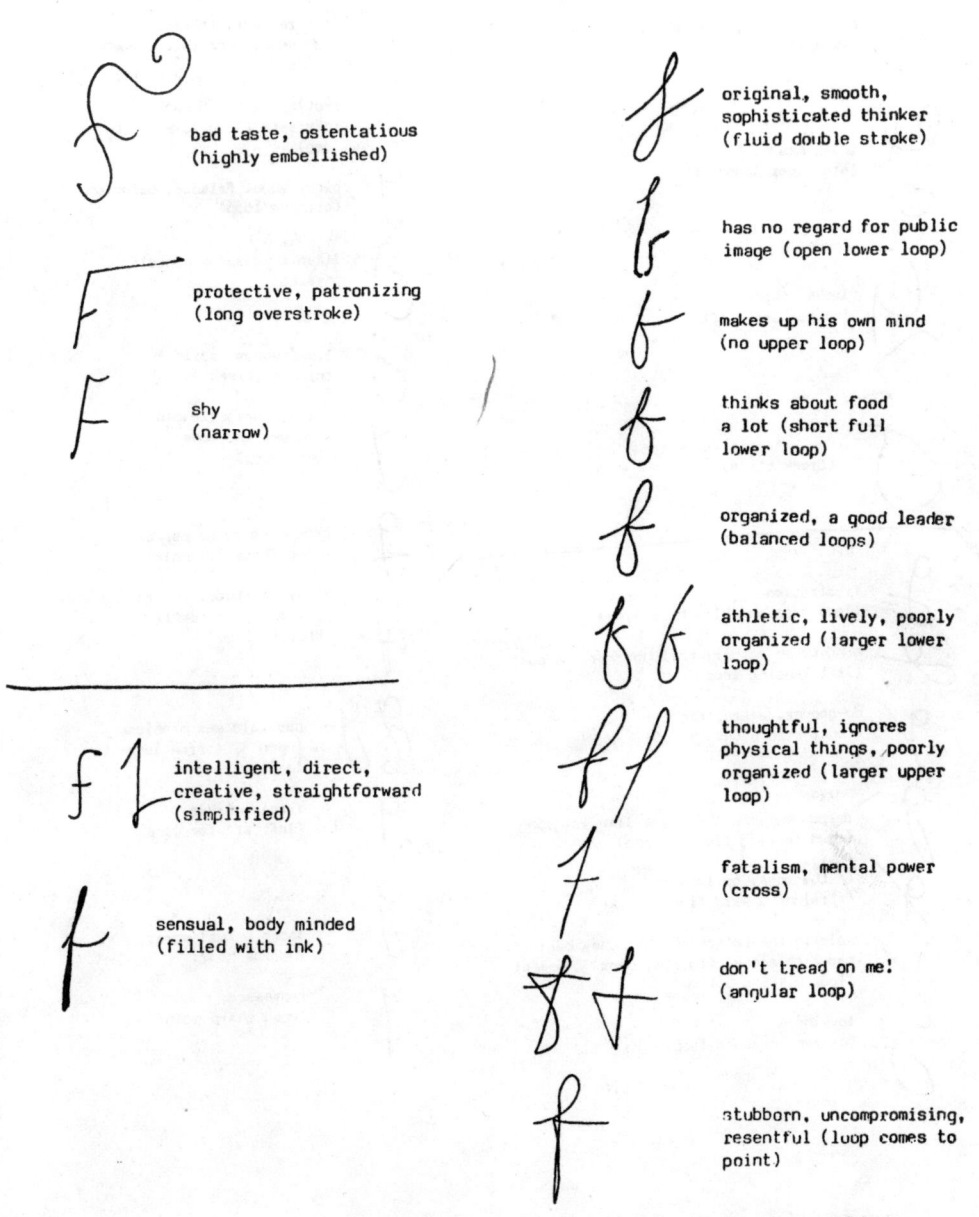

bad taste, ostentatious (highly embellished)

protective, patronizing (long overstroke)

shy (narrow)

intelligent, direct, creative, straightforward (simplified)

sensual, body minded (filled with ink)

original, smooth, sophisticated thinker (fluid double stroke)

has no regard for public image (open lower loop)

makes up his own mind (no upper loop)

thinks about food a lot (short full lower loop)

organized, a good leader (balanced loops)

athletic, lively, poorly organized (larger lower loop)

thoughtful, ignores physical things, poorly organized (larger upper loop)

fatalism, mental power (cross)

don't tread on me! (angular loop)

stubborn, uncompromising, resentful (loop comes to point)

G. G and Y are read the same. G centers on sex and physical relations. Y on money matters and materialism.

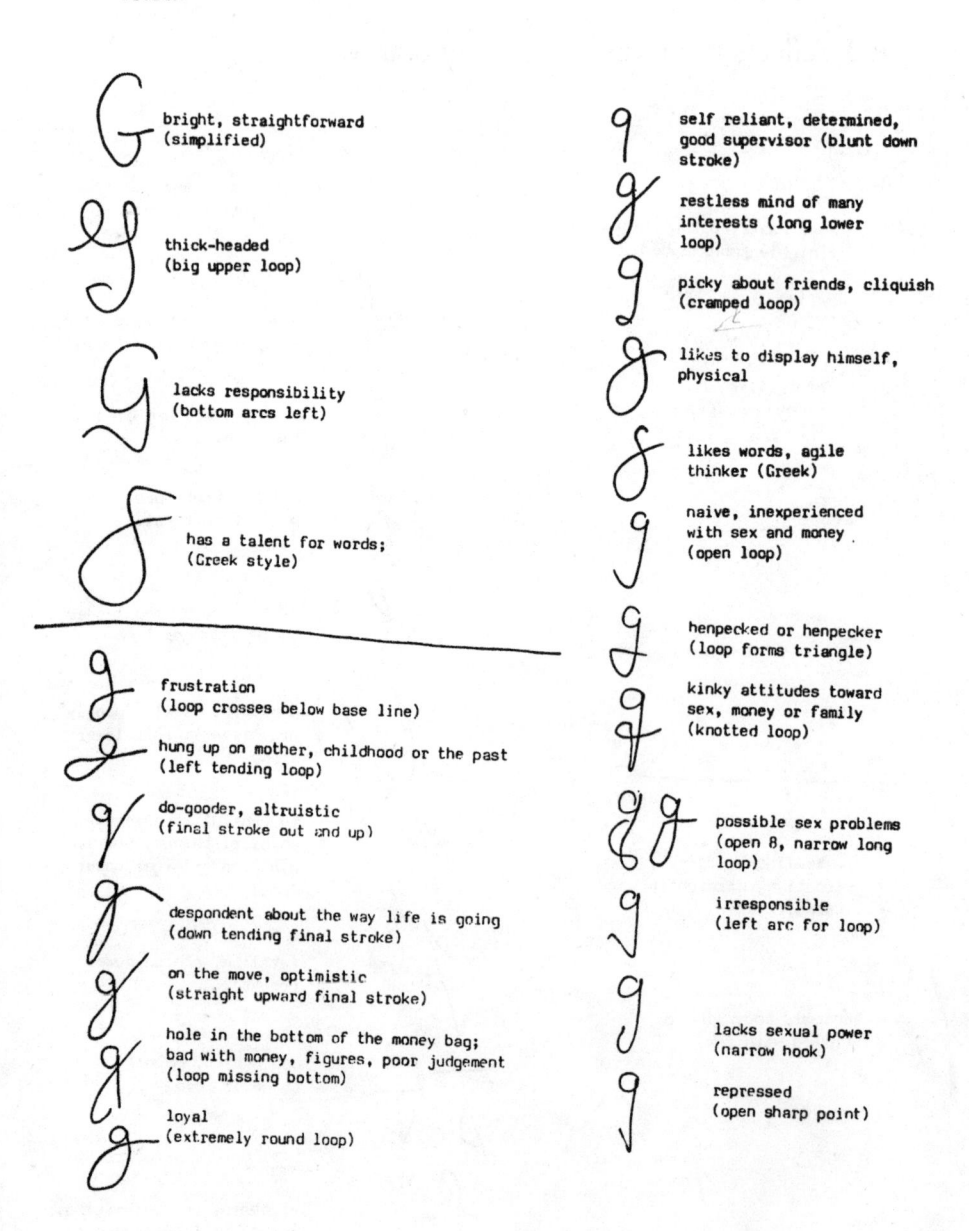

bright, straightforward
(simplified)

thick-headed
(big upper loop)

lacks responsibility
(bottom arcs left)

has a talent for words;
(Greek style)

---

frustration
(loop crosses below base line)

hung up on mother, childhood or the past
(left tending loop)

do-gooder, altruistic
(final stroke out and up)

despondent about the way life is going
(down tending final stroke)

on the move, optimistic
(straight upward final stroke)

hole in the bottom of the money bag;
bad with money, figures, poor judgement
(loop missing bottom)

loyal
(extremely round loop)

self reliant, determined,
good supervisor (blunt down stroke)

restless mind of many interests (long lower loop)

picky about friends, cliquish
(cramped loop)

likes to display himself, physical

likes words, agile thinker (Greek)

naive, inexperienced with sex and money
(open loop)

henpecked or henpecker
(loop forms triangle)

kinky attitudes toward sex, money or family
(knotted loop)

possible sex problems
(open 8, narrow long loop)

irresponsible
(left arc for loop)

lacks sexual power
(narrow hook)

repressed
(open sharp point)

H. H is a mental letter.

H   intelligent, confident
(simplified)

H H   shy
(narrow)

H   Harry Houdini's H; knows
how to get out of tight spots

h   spiritually aware
(high round loop)

h   won't compromise, stubborn
(leftward downstroke)

h   not intelligent, poor
spiritual values
(short upper loop)

h   strong opinions, rigid moral
standards
(high narrow loop)

I. Small **i** reflects the writer's talent for detail and wrapping things up. The dot is the most important part. The capital **I** shows the writer's feelings about himself and his feelings toward parents.

dreamer, imaginative
(high dot)

impatient, enthusiastic, likes curious things
(flying dot)

pays attention to detail, precise
(round dot, just above stem)

careless, absent minded
(no dot)

wants attention, non conformist, hates routine, faddish, perhaps frustrated
(circle dot)

neurotic
(dot open to left)

pays attention, notices surroundings
(dot open to right)

sarcastic
(flying v dot)

critical, hard to please
(tent dot)

evaluates everyone, judgemental, finds fault easily
(angle dot open to right)

stalls, tries to avoid tough decisions
(dot left of stem)

easily fired up, but also easily irritated
(dash to right of stem)

materialistic, builder
(square dot)

84

mechanically inclined, constructive, steady, able and willing
(simple, printed)

independent, mature, knows own worth, clear thinker
(straight line)

mother has influence over writer
(full upper, incomplete lower loop)

father has influence over writer
(full lower, incomplete upper)

doesn't like to talk about himself, repressed, shy
(upper loop retraced)

likes to talk about himself
(big upper loop)

puts himself down
(capital I smaller than other letters)

doesn't like others
(both loops unfinished)

self critical, introvert
(left leaning, especially in right leaning writing)

social, outgoing
(right leaning)

self centered; puts himself before anyone
(far right leaning)

rocking chair I; observer but not participant; loves father but doesn't feel up to expectations
(wide, unadorned bottom loop, unfinished)

forceful, can face problems with father
(knot in second loop)

candle flame; consuming intellect

stiff necked, idealistic
(tall loop)

irresponsible
(left arc for loop)

self critical, anti-social, resentful
(angular)

disinterested, takes the easy solution
(single curve)

sees his parents as money sources
(dollar sign)

85

J. The loops on **J** are read like those of **G** and **Y**. A small **j** is read like an **i** dot, combined with a **g** loop.

K. **K** deals largely with social and worldly relationships.

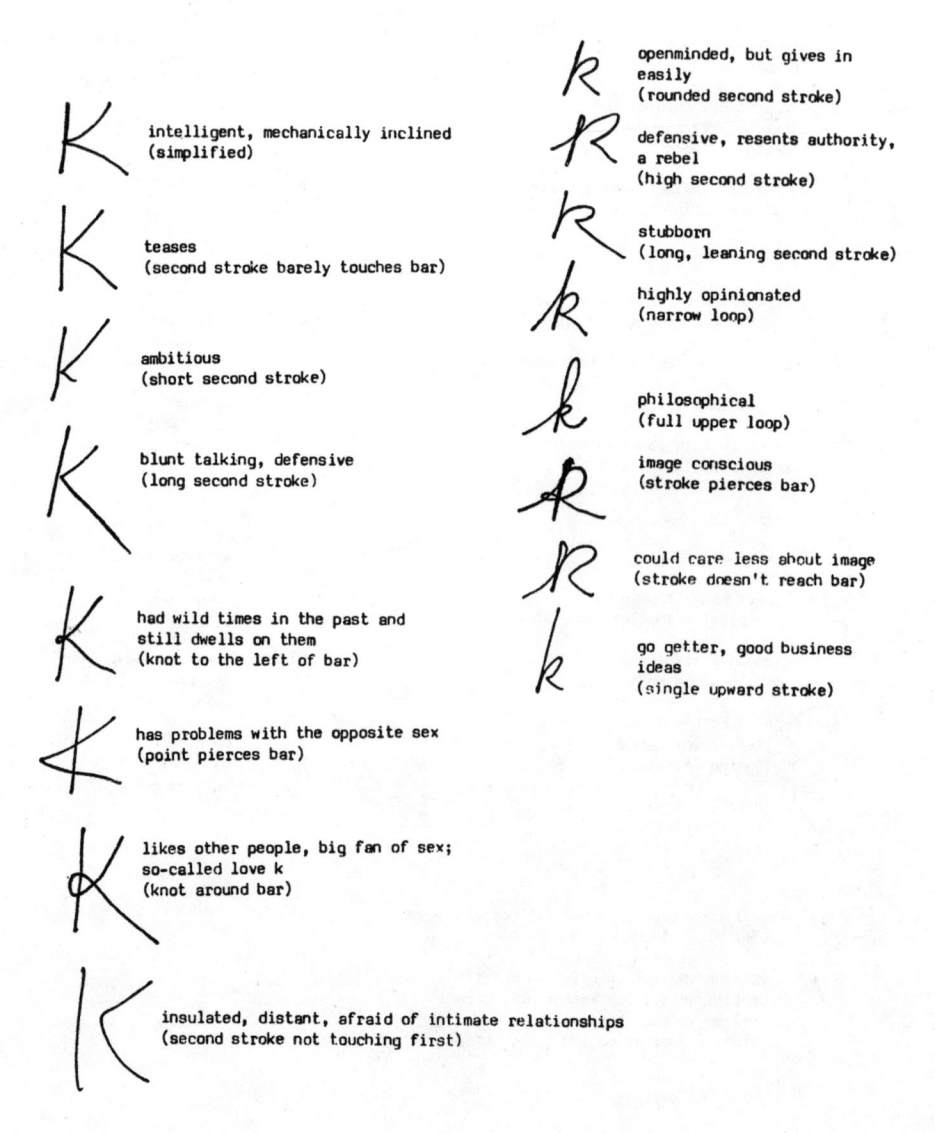

K intelligent, mechanically inclined
(simplified)

K teases
(second stroke barely touches bar)

K ambitious
(short second stroke)

K blunt talking, defensive
(long second stroke)

K had wild times in the past and still dwells on them
(knot to the left of bar)

K has problems with the opposite sex
(point pierces bar)

K likes other people, big fan of sex; so-called love k
(knot around bar)

K insulated, distant, afraid of intimate relationships
(second stroke not touching first)

k openminded, but gives in easily
(rounded second stroke)

k defensive, resents authority, a rebel
(high second stroke)

k stubborn
(long, leaning second stroke)

k highly opinionated
(narrow loop)

k philosophical
(full upper loop)

k image conscious
(stroke pierces bar)

k could care less about image
(stroke doesn't reach bar)

k go getter, good business ideas
(single upward stroke)

L. L is a letter of mental attitude.

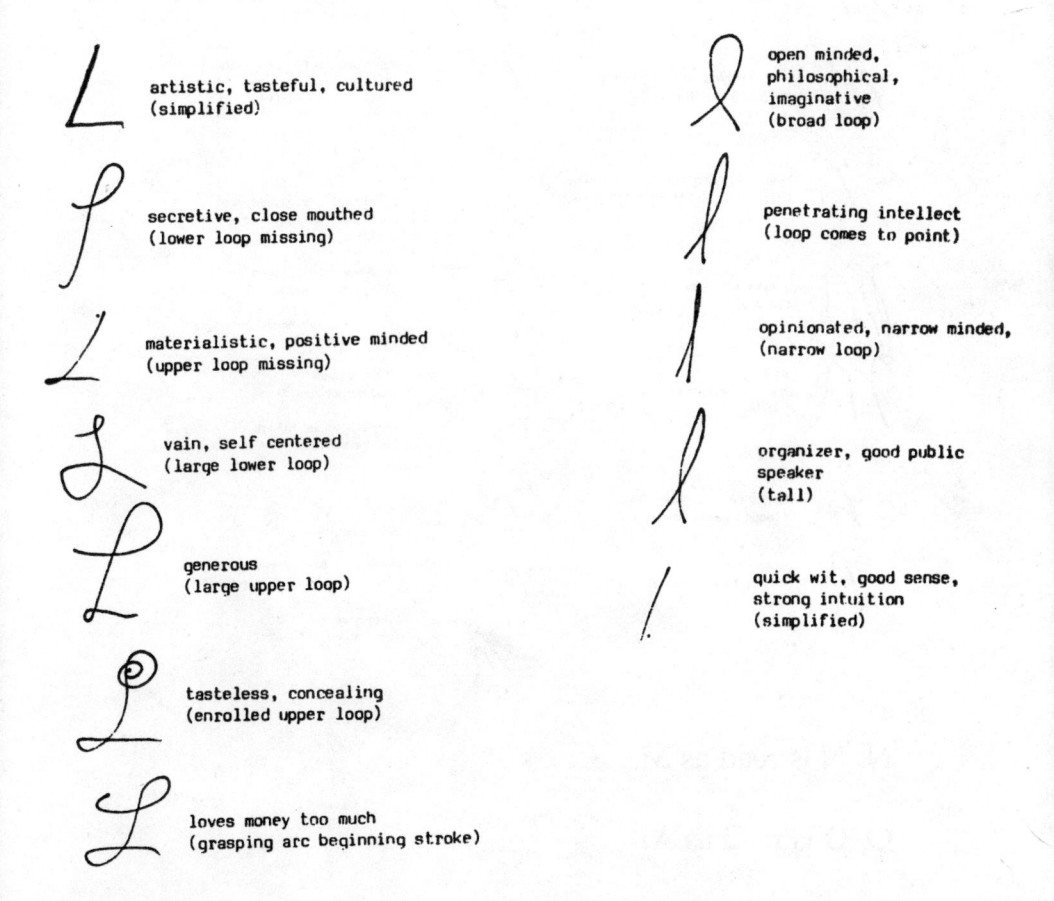

artistic, tasteful, cultured
(simplified)

secretive, close mouthed
(lower loop missing)

materialistic, positive minded
(upper loop missing)

vain, self centered
(large lower loop)

generous
(large upper loop)

tasteless, concealing
(enrolled upper loop)

loves money too much
(grasping arc beginning stroke)

open minded,
philosophical,
imaginative
(broad loop)

penetrating intellect
(loop comes to point)

opinionated, narrow minded,
(narrow loop)

organizer, good public
speaker
(tall)

quick wit, good sense,
strong intuition
(simplified)

M. **M** touches on many areas.

immature, envious, unsure of self
(third stroke high)

makes best of a bad situation,
condescends
(tapering to right)

tactless
(short center strokes)

measures people, shrewd, demands proof
(narrow)

rude, offensive
(second stroke peaked)

fierce temper, love of gambling
(sharp beginning stroke)

cheat, untrustworthy, underhanded
(horizontal sharp beginning)

worries about self
(lower loops in capital)

jealous
(small horizontal loop or box)

tries to hide worry
(looped first stroke)

dishonest
(incomplete third stroke)

pleasant nature, good sense of humor
(curved beginning)

caustic, dry wit
(horizontal beginning)

pride in family, but also possible doubts, secrets about himself
(inward curve)

interested only in essentials
(block printed)

loves responsibility and money
(beginning vertical loop)

socially ambitious, values opinions of friends rather than general public
(high second stroke)

likes to work with hands, gentle, analytical
(rounded)

quick thinker, likes mental tasks, sorts facts well
(peaked)

temperamental, finds fault
(final stroke pointed)

under stress, accident prone
(extra loop)

clairvoyance
(upper strokes looped)

worries about others
(lower strokes looped)

proud
(flag beginning stroke)

repressed but shrewd
(final stroke left tending)

likes possessions
(beginning left arc)

N. **N** is read as **M**.

O. **O** is read as **A**.

P. P relates to the amount of physical activity.

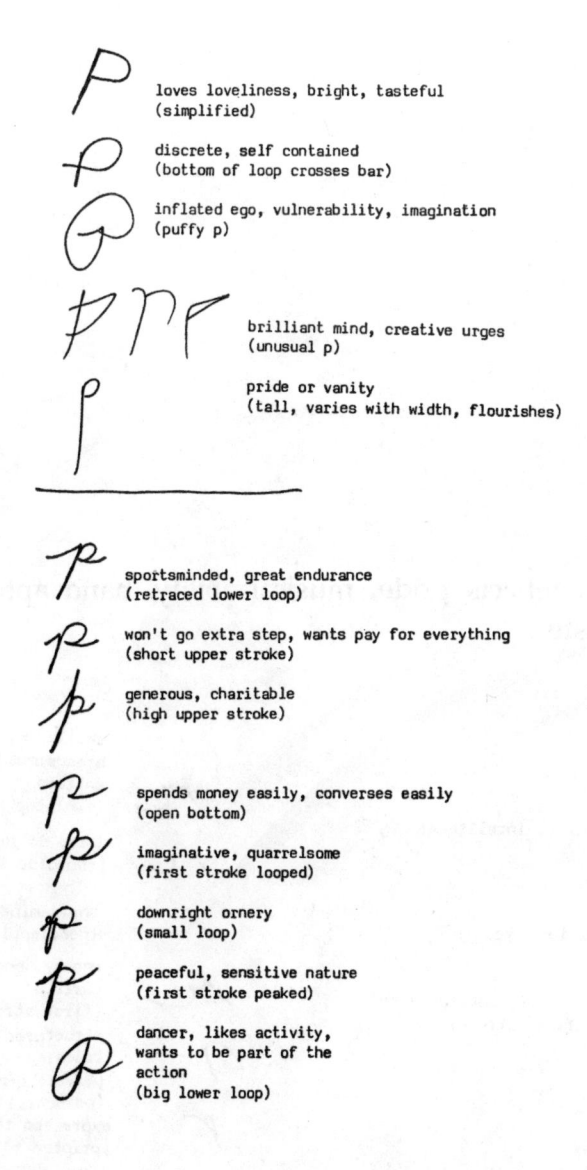

loves loveliness, bright, tasteful
(simplified)

discrete, self contained
(bottom of loop crosses bar)

inflated ego, vulnerability, imagination
(puffy p)

brilliant mind, creative urges
(unusual p)

pride or vanity
(tall, varies with width, flourishes)

---

sportsminded, great endurance
(retraced lower loop)

won't go extra step, wants pay for everything
(short upper stroke)

generous, charitable
(high upper stroke)

spends money easily, converses easily
(open bottom)

imaginative, quarrelsome
(first stroke looped)

downright ornery
(small loop)

peaceful, sensitive nature
(first stroke peaked)

dancer, likes activity,
wants to be part of the action
(big lower loop)

Q. The top of **Q** is read like **A**, the bottom like a **g** or **y** loop.

R. **R** reflects pride, musical ability, hand aptitude, and taste.

R   likes literature, intelligent
(simplified)

R   ambitious
(short second stroke)

R   hunger for success, enterprising
(upreaching first stroke)

⌐   skilled with tools, broadminded about spiritual matters
(tabletop r)

∩   dull, doesn't pay attention
(rounded, lazy r)

∧   sharp mind, observant
(needlepoint r)

r   choosy, good visual perception, curious
(first stroke higher)

r   structured thinking, follows rules, probably went to private school
(parochial r)

r   expresses thoughts easily
(printed r)

⋀   dexterity in both hands
(two peaks)

ℓ   sings in the shower
(looped first stroke)

S. S is an attitude letter.

cultured, tasteful; if printed, building ability, mechanical aptitude (simplified)

likes music, may have musical ability (treble clef)

shies from responsibility (left arc)

nice fellow, but mentally sloppy (one stroke, lazy s)

artistic temperament (snake-like)

digs for the facts, stubborn about ideas (comes to a peak)

gives in easily (rounded top)

secretive (closed loop)

greedy, clever (enrolled)

tough, hangs on (lower loop)

plays by the rules (small capital)

imagination (loop stop main body)

T. Different parts of T point up social openness, idealism, will power, goal strength, self-control, and details of mental outlook.

protective
(crossbar extends to right)

bad taste and attachment to the past
(ornate crossbar and left tending strokes)

doesn't express himself well, repressed
(retraced stem)

talkative, articulate but thin skinned
(loop stem)

stubborn, holds grudges
(stiff beginning stroke)

lofty goals, idealistic
(tall stem)

loner, cautious, timid
(short stem)

lazy, slow poked
(two-part stem)

enthusiastic
(long crossbar)

sarcastic, cruel at times
(long and sharp crossbar)

mentally agile, effective planner
(one crossbar for two t's)

doesn't live up to potential, lacks control, will power
(short crossbar)

tries for self-control, to overcome instincts
(bowed crossbar)

works to overcome desire to put things off
(left bowed crossbar)

superficial thinker, good sense of humor, easy going
(shallow dish crossbar)

sensible, feels responsible
(star t)

avoids competition, lacks willpower, vitality
(light pressure)

indecisive, quitter
(beginning heavy pressure that fades)

self-controlled, firm
(heavy pressure)

daydreamer, easily bothered
(crossbar above stem)

sees far ahead, high aspirations, proud, able and idealistic, a mover
(high crossbar)

keeps goals within his grasp, organized, careful, accurate
(balanced crossbar)

doubts his abilities, puny goals, takes orders, feels inferior
)low crossbar)

U. **U** is read as an upside-down **N**.

V. **V** reflects emotional intensity.

solid intellect, straightforward attitude
(simplified)

doesn't like authority, succeeds when left
to pursue own ideas
(high second stroke)

concerned about and protective of
others
(long final stroke)

resists outside influenc(e)
(angular)

looking inward,
uncommunicative
(retraced lines)

cares about appearances,
uncertain
(arcade beginning)

depressed, suicidal tendencies
(final stroke curves back through letter)

fearful of involvement
(arcade final stroke)

W. **W** points up likes and dislikes.

clear minded, intelligent, artistic
(simplified)

lover of beauty
(curved and sharp strokes)

sense of humor
(wavy beginning stroke)

poetic
(loop on final stroke)

analytical thinker
(angular)

fears the years ahead,
hides in the past
(curved in on itself)

X. X is a letter of enterprise and adaptability.

precise, stand offish
        standoffish
(even cross)

bad feelings toward the past
(heavy downstroke to the left)

ambitious
(high right stroke)

labors for the future
(curve and line)

has problems changing, talkative
(two uncrossed lines)

Y. Y is read as G.

Z. Z made with a lower loop is read as G or Y.

Signature

Once you have analyzed the writing in your sample, turn your attention to your signature.

Your signature represents all the things about your personality you want to emphasize to the world. It is your most concentrated statement of personal feelings.

The signatures of most self-confident people are rather simple. Their regular handwriting and their signatures tend to look alike, because their personalities require no more dramatic statement of existence.

For others, however, the signature is a place where ego and other deeply held personal feelings can prance into the limelight, making the writer feel the way he wishes the world would treat him. That is what makes name signing so satisfying.

Examine your signature with all the tools you've used on the rest of your writing, plus these additional ones:

The larger the capital letters in your signature the greater your ego drive for success. An enlarged capital on the last name indicates extreme pride in family.

John Jones

Capitals that are smaller than the other signature letters imply deep feelings of self-worthlessness.

thad wilson

Placement of the signature is important, too. If it is at the right-hand margin, no significance is attached. But the closer it lies to the left margin, the greater the degree of unhappiness and depression. Suicide notes often have signatures at the far left edge.

Extending an overstroke over the signature indicates high intellectual or spiritual goals. A long understroke shows pride in the balance, poise, and control the writer has attained.

A vertically extended signature indicates the desire for a distinctive reputation. The higher the extension the greater the distinction desired.

A dot placed at the end of the signature means the writer guards himself against others. He doens't trust anyone but himself.

Melvin Berman.

The more threadlike the signature, the better the writer will be at solving complex problems.

Lewis Randolph

And a signature that gets smaller as it goes along, indicates a shrewd, diplomatic personality.

SECTION THREE:

How About a Handwriting Party?

Once you've practiced on yourself and a few close friends you should be ready for a handwriting party.

Here's what you'll need to hold one:
1. Lots of different kinds of pens.
2. Plenty of plain white paper.
3. An emotion wheel drawn onto tracing paper.
4. Lined paper for judging line slant and zones.
5. A magnifying glass for examining small writing and tiny features.
6. The graphology review sheet included with this section.
7. A large pad of paper, like an art sketchpad, for drawing examples on large enough for everyone to see.

The best way to run a handwriting party, so that all of the attention isn't on you (that's not much fun for guests), is to let everyone analyze their own writing under your direction. It would take days for you to examine the writing of all your guests, and it would be boring, too.

By using what you've learned to lead the others along, you create a happy group activity that everyone will be interested in.

Let your party begin like any get-together. Have records, snacks, drinks. Let everyone get relaxed and into the party mood before you begin the handwriting session.

When you start, give everyone paper and let them choose a pen. Having a pen they like is important. Ask them all to write three or four sentences about anything they wish. Have magazines or books handy for writing on if there aren't enough tables available. Then ask them all to sign their papers.

Using the review sheet, lead them through a simple graphology exam. When it's over have everyone say what their analysis revealed about them. Some of the results will be serious, a few will be hilarious.

I guarantee that, with all the interesting things your friends will discover in their writing, you'll have the liveliest party ever.

Once you have many readings under your belt, you can try entertaining at other people's parties for pay. (It probably won't be much, but it will be exciting and fun.)

All you'll need—besides the experience and confidence to analyze in front of strangers—are some circulars announcing your act. Post them in local supermarkets and restaurants. Send them to area church social groups and neighborhood centers. Drop them by schools, clubs, and the families of all your friends and relatives.

A sample circular is included here to give you a guide for making your own.

Announcing:
an Exciting Entertainment for your next party or meeting

GRAPHOLOGY
The Secrets of Writing, Revealed!

THE AMAZING
Your Name Here
will
UNLOCK
the secrets of writing for you!
CALL Today

INEXPENSIVE   Your Phone Number   **FASCINATING**

Handwriting Party Review Sheet

These are the basic points to cover when leading your friends through an handwriting analysis. Since this is for social event, we'll keep the reading simple, looking only at the general patterns of writing, not at individual letters.

1. Point out that handwriting shows a person's personality in the same way as the kind of artwork he likes, but much more clearly and deeply. Handwriting analysis doesn't predict, it reveals facts the writer has hidden in his writing.

2. Ask them to write at least six lines of whatever comes into their heads, except poetry.

3. Zones. Show them the lined paper, explain what zones are. Remember, the upper zone reflects intellect and imagination; the middle zone shows the day-to-day person; the lower zone deals with urges, drives, and compulsions. The more activity in the zone, the more important that area of life. The more flourished the activity, the more creative or wild the writer's attitudes in that area.

4. Slant. Show your guests the emotion wheel. Explain how they should line it up with a line of their writing. Tell them to mark which letter slant best matches their writing. When everyone is done, review the meanings. A is practical, easy going, independent, and dependable. B is a people-person: confident, impulsive, open to influence. C is the wide open, intense, expressive, sensitive, volatile person. D is the thoughtful, cold, picky, unsocial person—more brains than personality. E is a person repressing deep emotions, defiant, and uncomfortable in crowds.

5. Line Direction. Point out that if the whole line slants up, the writer is optimistic. Down slating means pessimistic or tired. No slant shows dependability, but maybe dullness, too. An arc shows a racer who tires before the finish. A dish means a turtle who keeps going after a slow start.

6. Strokes. Draw examples of garlands, arcades, angles, and threads on your example pad. Review the meanings for your guests: Garland denotes adaptability, sympathy, outgoing personality. Arcades show self-centeredness and superficiality. Angles are signs of rigidity, high ideals. Threads are written by folks with insight, wit, and great adaptability.

7. Spacing. Tell your friends that spacing is our mind's unconscious way of expressing our attitudes toward society. Small spacing implies chattiness, confidence, trust; if small but uneven, add insecurity. Large spacing is the sign of an introvert—a thoughtful, literary person; if uneven, add timidness and difficulty in expression. Talk about line spacing: narrow implies spontaneity; wide denotes organizational and reasonableness; very wide means remoteness, a desire to be alone. Tangles imply impulsive and overinterest in whatever zone they occur in.

8. Margin. Without getting too involved, tell your guests that margins show conscious attitudes toward tolerance, economy, consistency, and social acceptance. The top margin reflects formality. The wider, the more formal. The bottom reveals sensuality. This time the wide, the less sensual. The left margin reflects the need for esteem; narrower means greater. The right shows how close the writer actually likes people to be; again, narrower means greater.

9. Pressure. Briefly point out that pressure shows the writer's emotional power. Light pressure comes from

sensitive, shy people; heavy pressure from people who are dynamic or who have a deep emotional tie to what they are writing. Note pasty writing and draw or pass around an example. Explain how it points out high intelligence. artistic sense, and other good qualities.

10. Writing size. There are four main types: tall, small, wide, and narrow. Show examples on your pad of each type. Tall writing shows a person aiming for the stars. Small writing comes from someone who examines everything in life in detail. Wide writing implies a person who needs lots of personal space. Narrow writing comes from a person who feels hemmed in by life.

11. Simplification. Explain that simplification that remains readable shows intelligence. Fragmented writing, however, which is simplified past readability, is the mark of a degenerate personality. Enrichment, on the other hand, shows a person who loves art and beauty.

12. Signature. Tell your group how the signature is their expression of how they want the world to view them. Go over the basic areas of study and show your guests how to relate them to a signature. Inform them of the importance of signature placement. The closer to the left margin, the more emotional problems. Also, capital letter height reflects pride in a name.

13. Ask for questions. Have the book handy to cover any topics you aren't sure of. Encourage anyone whose writing doesn't fit the general pattern to check through the book for a detailed situation that might fit better.

14. Ask everyone what they think of the analysis. Have them recite what they've found in their own writings. Try to get everyone talking about their personalities and feelings. Once you get this started, your party should stay interesting for hours.

SECTION FOUR:

Analyzing the Famous and the Infamous

Here is a final challenge of your graphology skills. The samples shown here come from famous and infamous people. Can you tell which are which?

It is impossible, through graphology, to figure out the names of the writers. But a skillful analysis can tell quite clearly the **kind** of people they are.

A hint: These fragments were written by a President, the killer of a President, a great female scientist, a great male scientist, a famous novelist and a famous artist, both of whom committed suicide, and an illustrious explorer.

Can you figure out which is which? If you're feeling confident, take a stab at the names. You'll find them on pages 111-113.

„San Francisco de Paula, Cuba do hereby make, publish and declare this instrument as my Last Will and TESTAMENT ‚in manner following‚ that is to say:
.I. I hereby cancel, annul, and revoke all wills and codicils by me at any time heretofore made;
2. I hereby give, devise and bequeath to my beloved

Liebe Mutter!

Heute eine freudige Nachricht. H. A. Lorentz hat mir telegraphiert, dass die englischen Expeditionen die Lichtablenkung an der Sonne wirklich bewiesen haben. Maja schreibt mir leider, dass Du nicht nur viel Schmerzen hast, sondern dass Du Dir auch noch trübe Gedanken machest. Wie gern würde

But, in a larger sense, we can not dedicate— we can not consecrate— we can not hallow— this ground. The brave men, living and dead, who struggled here, have consecrated it, far above our poor power to add or detract. The world will little note, nor long remember, what we say here, but it can never forget what they did here. It is for us, the living, rather, to be dedicated here to the unfinished work which they who fought here, have, thus far, so nobly advanced. It is rather for us to be here dedicated to the great task remaining before

Aux yeux charmés tout offre un ravissant spectacle
Le modeste fossé brille plus qu'un trésor
Le ciel éblouissant, tamisé par les branches

...... I wish to protest against this action,
...... and against the conduct of the officials of
...... the United States consular service who
...... acted on behalf of the United States
...... government.

Sendaeme podziwisanie od Ireneme
oddanej

(Sketch given us by Yel-
=lept the principal Cheif of
the Wallahwollah Nation.)

SECTION FIVE:

For More Information

If you'd like to learn more about graphology and the secrets locked into handwriting, I'd start by writing the worldwide organization of graphologists:

The International Grapho-Analysis Society
325 W. Jackson Blvd.
Chicago, Il 60606

Ask them for literature and for the names and addresses of graphologists in your area. Perhaps one of them will let you assist him or will teach you the finer points of handwriting analysis.

Many books have been written on graphology. Rather than spending a lot of money buying most of them, I'd look in the library. Many of the best books are currently out of print and most are hard to find and expensive.

I will recommend one book highly. If you are serious about learning graphology, you should order it, because it can serve as both a practice manual and a reference. Happily, it only costs $4.95:

A Graphology Student's Workbook
by Ruth Gardner
Llewellyn Publications
PO Box 3383
St. Paul, Minnesota 55165

INDEX

Alphabet 75-94
Angle strokes 36, 38, 105
Arcade Strokes 36, 37, 105
Astrology 8

Baudelaire, (Pierre) Charles 12
Beginning Strokes 38-43
BIC Banana pens 63
Browning, Robert 12
Bunker, Milton 14

Capital letters 70-71, 96
Connective Strokes 36-38, 105

Demelles, Francis 12

Emotion wheel chart 29, 105
Ending strokes 43-48

Flandrin, Abbe 13

Gardner, Ruth 116
Garland strokes 36-37, 105
Goethe, Johann 12
Graphologists 9, 14-15, 116
Graphology 8-10, 12ff *See also*
    handwriting
  books 12-13, 116
  definition 8-9
  Germany as center 13-14
  in business 15
  in crime detection 14-15
  organizations 15, 116
  word invented 13
Graphology Student's Workbook, A 116

Handwritng. *See also* graphology
　analysis 9-10, 17ff.
　definition 9
　dominant themes 18
　enrichment 73-74, 107
　fragmentary 74, 107
　margins 53-62, 106
　personality clues 7-10, 12-15, 18, 20ff.
　pressure 63-66, 106-107
　samples 110-113
　scientific study 12-14
　simplification 72-73, 107
　size 67-71, 107
　slant 28-36, 105
　　degree 28-31
　　directional trend 31-32
　　line direction 32-36, 105
　spacing 49-52, 106
　strokes 36-48, 105
　zones 19-28, 51, 104
Handwriting party 100-108
　review sheet 104-108
　sample circular 103
Hauptman, Bruno 14

I-Ching 8
International Grapho-Analysis Society, The 15, 116

Keats, John 12
Klages, Dr. Ludwig 13

Lindbergh, Charles 14

Lives of the Caesars 12
Loops 22-27

Margins 53-62, 106
Michon, Abbe 13

Nero 12
Numerology 8

Occult sciences 8

Scott, Sir Walter 13
Signatures 15, 95-98, 107
Slant 28-36, 105
   degree 28-31
   direction 31-36, 105
Spacing 49-52, 106
Strokes 36-48, 105
   beginning 38-48, 105
   connective 36-38, 105
     angle 36, 38, 105
     arcade 36-37, 105
     garland 36-37, 105
     thread 36, 38, 105
   ending 43-48

Tarot 8
Thread strokes 36, 38, 105

Werling, Father Norman 15

Zones 19-28, 51, 104

Robinson Township Library
Robinson, Illinois 62454

Robinson Township Library
Robinson, Illinois 62454

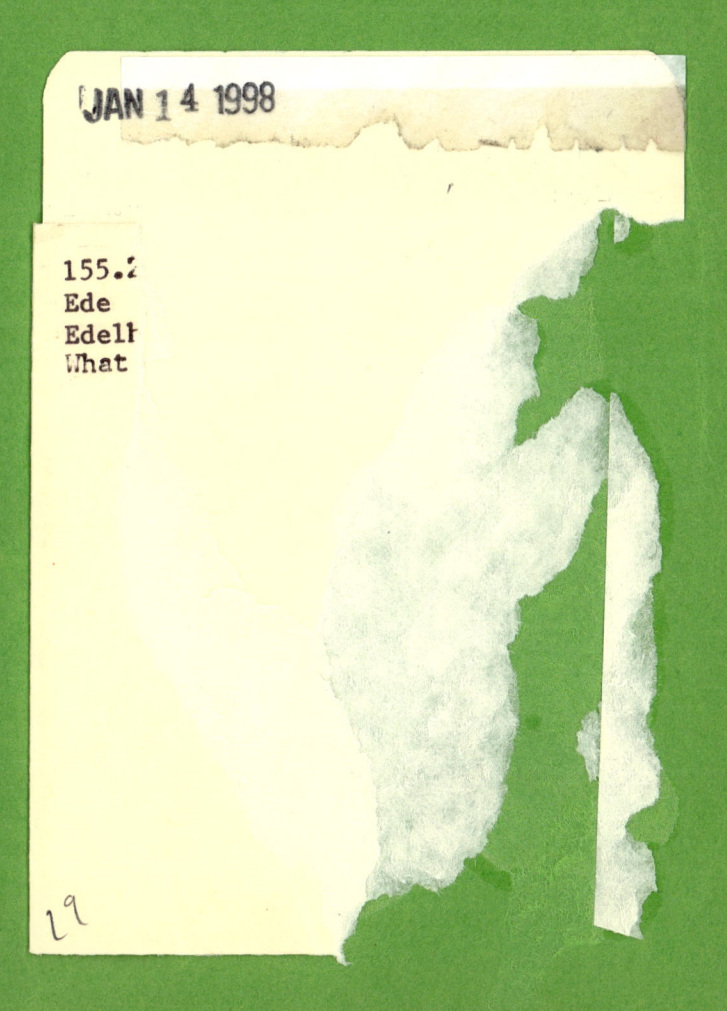

JAN 14 1998

155.2
Ede
Edelh
What

29